# The Leaking Heart

kim marie farris

*To my Mother,*

*As you are looking down*
*From the skies above*
*This is dedicated to you*
*With all my love.*

*As you open up these pages, you're opening up my heart, my soul, and experiences throughout many years of love, desperation, depression with suicidal thoughts, and hope.*

*I caution you, as you will read my raw, organic vulnerability: There is only so much that one can do to secure that delicate vital organ in their chest, and sometimes it leaks.*

*I present to you,* **The Leaking Heart.**

*I'm not giving up*
*I am just letting go*
*I am freeing myself*
*I'm digging deep to my soul*
*Bring out the light from within*
*The universe is on my side*
*I have faith, I believe*
*While I go through this process*
*I need a favor*
*Hold something for me*
*It has broken*
*It's been burned*
*And beaten up*
*It is scarred*
*Sewn together by a thread*
*I'm giving you this*
*Until I see you again*
*I trust you with my heart*
*Please take care of it*

# LOVE and LIGHT

You are my light at the end of the tunnel

When everything's in disarray


You are a splinter of sunshine

That brightens up my day


You are the hope that springs eternal

When I see no end in sight


You give me a reason to keep moving

Knowing everything will be all right


When I want to end it all

All I have to do


Is think of you

To keep me from the fall


You are the rainbow of color

When everything is blue

It puts a smile on my face

Just by hearing from you


You are the calming of the ocean

When the waves come crashing down


You are the peace to my mind and spirit

When there's so much chaos around


I think of your kindness and warmth

When I'm feeling all alone


You are my light at the end of the tunnel

With you I am home

Every waking moment

You are on my mind

I think of your eyes

Your smile

Your voice

Your gentle voice

Shining through

With one look

Without any words

You are genuine

You are real

Amongst chaos

You are my calm

Right now

At this moment

I need you

Your arms

To hold me

Your breath

To warm me

Your kiss

To soothe me

Your hands

To touch me

Your love

To heal me

There once was a girl

Who lived in a world

Which was always dismal and gray

She felt so lonely

And felt so insecure

She was sad almost everyday

Then a prince came along

And sang her a song

She couldn't believe it was true

But he held her hand

And kissed her deeply

And said, "I have a connection with you"

She thought he was bogus

Maybe a bit atrocious

But in her heart she believed him to be true

An unforgettable night

And as the moon shined bright

She knew she was forever changed

She woke the next morning

Loving the sun and its glory

Her thoughts were so rearranged

She was a new person inside

And just couldn't hide

What was buried deep within

She was beautiful and strong

The dismal gray was gone

Her new life would begin

She didn't see her prince

But she was quite convinced

One day they would meet again

What is it

That you do to me

How you change my world

Almost instantly

From darkness

And melancholy

To brightening my day

So wonderfully

I feel as I've known you

For thousands of years

You make me feel whole

And take away my fears

I don't remember how life was

Before I met you

We are in each other's lives for a reason

That I know is true

So no matter how many weeks

Or months we are apart

Know that you'll always and forever

Have a special place in my heart

I can't remember

Since I've smiled so much

I get a sense of invigoration

Just by the feel of your touch

I feel bad that my actions

Are blocked by fear

But it means so much

Just to have you near

I never met anyone

Quite like you

So patient and understanding

And allow my real self to shine through

Your tenderness and sense of humor

Gets me through my strife

I truly adore you

Thank you for coming in to my life

Never did I believe

I would feel like this

A warm hand to hold

Tender lips to kiss

It is hard to believe

I've found someone like you

I feel I am in a dream

That this cannot be true

Every day I am falling deeper

Than I ever knew I could

I feel I don't deserve you

I never thought I would

I want to forget about the past

And start everything new

I look forward to the future

And spending it with you

It's only you

Who warms my heart

I thank the heavens above

You are my shining star

It's you who

Puts the twinkle in my eye

And speaks words of sweetness

Bringing tears of happiness to my eyes

I love you

With all of my soul

It is with you

I want to grow old

Love has found a way

To keep us together

Through circumstance

And coincidence

The timing

The obstacles

Just bumps in the road

Emotions rooted deep within

Prevent any hardship to break

This beautiful bond

The universe is on our side

It's been a long time

since I've felt

anything

But you

make me feel

like something

I've never known

Passion

A cosmic connection

Time stops

Communication

Without words

Simple touch

Electrifying reaction

Nerves tingle

Heart races

Unison not with lips

With souls

Hypnotized

By your eyes

A touch of your hand

Sends shivers down my spine

An extended glance

We're caught in a trance

Time stands still

No one else has a chance

I want to kiss

Your sweet lips

Imagining that moment

Makes my heart skip

A caress of your face

A warm embrace

Heartbeat in my chest

Increasing in pace

I want to envelop

My love around you

Go to your darkest places

Go deep in to your soul

Remove all insecurities

Banish all fear

Know you inside and out

And fall in love with you

Even more

When life gets crazy

And all seems too much

I slow myself down

And think of your touch

I think of the moment

Your hand was in mine

Looking in to your eyes

And getting lost in time

I think of your embrace

So warm and strong

Your arms wrapped around me

Holding each other for so long

This keeps me going

When I feel all alone

Giving me something

To look forward to

When you're finally home

Overwhelmed with emotion

Yet calm in my thoughts

Of you


The vulnerability

The openness and honesty


Your passion

Burning inside


Your soul

Hurting

Reaching

For something

Someone


To keep you

From going under


Take my hand

A lifeline

I open my heart

Pull you inside

Feel safe

Embracing our souls


In darkness

And in light

Always

Forever

My love

My muse

When things go astray

I think of you

My mind

My body

Feels at ease

I think of your eyes

Your smile

Your voice

Whispering softly in my ear

The warmth

Of your energy

I think of you

Even apart

If I can't have you

With me

You are here

In soul

In spirit

In my mind

And through me

How I long to have

A night with you

To talk

To laugh

To smile

Listen to your voice

As you tell your stories

The touch of your hand

How our eyes lock

No interruptions

Or time constraints

Be ourselves

Freedom

Relaxations

Only you

And I

Alone

Together

Only you
Make my heart flutter

Only you
Melts me like butter

Only you
Can make angels shudder

Only you
Make me feel like no other

Only you
I want to be with forever

It has been so long

Since I've felt like this

What I wish for

Is your sweet tender kiss

To feel your caresses

Brush softly against my cheek

Causing such exhilaration

And my knees to go weak

I want to hold you close

And feel your heart next to mine

Hear nothing but our hearts beat

Until the end of time

I want to talk to him

But I don't know what to say

I miss him so much

But he is so far away

I lie awake at night

And silently pray

He isn't working too hard

That he is ok

I look forward to seeing him

I can't wait for the day

To hold him and kiss him

And he tells me he'll stay…


With me.

# DARKNESS and DESPAIR

Be careful of what you see

When you look into her eyes

She may look like the devil

But she's an angel in disguise

Longing for the love

She so desperately deserves

Hiding behind a shield

Afraid of being hurt

Trying to pretend nothing is wrong

To forget about all of the pain

To have a positive outlook

So she can be happy again

But it doesn't seem so easy

To push it all aside

It only ends a backfire

Eating her up inside

Don't share anything

Keep it all inside

You'll get used to it

It will become easy to hide

Don't let anyone else see

What you truly feel

Just keep a smile on your face

And they'll think it's real

Could I have had you?

If I stayed a little longer

If I had embraced a little stronger


Could I have had you?

If I didn't shy of your advance

If I told you I was in a trance


Could I have had you?

If I let all inhibitions go

If I was strong and let you know


Could I have had you?

If I wasn't blind to see

Because you already had me

My heart is aching

Like it hasn't for a while

I'm filled with insecurity

Just like a little child

I don't understand this feeling

I don't understand why

But I found I'm attracted to you

And it makes me want to cry

I don't want to feel this way

Mainly because I am scared

I'm afraid to be hurt again

Or to find you just don't care

I need to get this feeling

Away from my beating heart

But I can't escape these feelings

It's tearing me apart

I look in the mirror and what do I see

A disfigured girl staring back at me

I see other girls so happy and thin

I would do anything to look just like them

I'm very unhappy; I try not to show

What I do is a secret, no one should know

I've lost several inches, in just a few weeks

I am still unsatisfied of the image I see

So I try even harder, purge and then starve

I never thought I would get this far

My clothes are loose, but my heart is tight

I'm losing control and putting up a fight

My muscles are weak; my head is weary

The only pound to shed comes from a tear

I need some help before it's too late

I've got a life to live; heaven can wait

I hate myself

I hate my life

All I wanted

Was to be someone's wife


To be a mother

To be a friend

To have children

My love would never end


I feel like

All I want to do is die

I have no worth

In anyone's life


I'm here just to serve

Like a robotic drone

No wonder I feel

Always so alone

I'm not meant to be happy

Or deserving of love

Although I pray silently

To God up above


I'm so scared and sad

Can it get any worse?

I just want it to end

Unless hope gets to me first

Life as I know it

Is passing me by

Makes me want to

Bury my head and cry


I compare myself

To family and friends

And people I barely know

Who are doing better than


I want to stop time

I want to escape

To start my life over

Instead of living in shame


I know there must be

A better way

To turn my life around

And make it okay

I'm tired of self-loathing

And thoughts of death

So many times

Of losing my breath


I don't know what to do

I feel as if I'm trapped

Filled with tension and anger

That my neck could snap

I want to be happy

I want to be loved

I want to believe

I was sent from above

I don't know where I'm going

I feel as if I'm standing still

Waiting for something

To give me my fill

I know I am meant for something

But no idea what it is

It is a feeling deep inside me

An extrasensory gift

What is it that has to happen

To change my life around

What do I need to do

To make myself proud?

I'm tired of being unhappy

I don't know what to change

How much of my life

Has to be rearranged

I'm in a downward spiral

And I feel it's getting worse

I am blocked from climbing up

As if I am under some kind of curse

It is affecting my health

My job, even my hair

I just want to escape

Any place, any where

I'm losing my enthusiasm

I'm losing my drive

But luckily there's still a spark

That I'll get through this, that I'll survive

What do I do to change?

I need some serious help

To rid of all these feelings forever

And finally love myself

I have a confession

It's a constant obsession

With every breath

I think of death

The only solution to my resolution

I am scared; I am frightened

I need my self-worth heightened

I can barely do my job

My head is in darkened fog

I am on the verge of tears

Bottling up all my fears

Who do I turn to, where do I go?

What is happening to me, I just don't know

I wake up depressed

And I don't know why

All I feel like doing

Is curl up and cry

I don't understand these feelings

Lethargic and weak

My laziness and avoidance

All I want to do is sleep

I wake up in a daze

Very slow and always late for work

I get stressed and more distracted

Which only makes it worse

I think I know the remedy

If I could crawl out of this rut

Some exercise and some reading

Something to really kick my butt

If there is one thing

I want in my life right now

Is to have a love of my own

I'm sick and tired

Of staying home at night

And feeling so alone

If I can stick around

For one more day

And watch the sun

Descend and melt away

Into the ocean

So large and vast

While I stand there

Thinking of my regretful past

Wondering what happened

What went wrong

Where have the last

Ten years of mine gone

So much wasted time

So much confusion

Moving place to place

As if in delusion

I can affect the future

I can't change the past

Start living for today

For positive outcomes to last

There is something

Missing from my life

Is the simple touch of love

To last me through the night

He doesn't have to be beside me

To know that he's always there

Just knowing he thinks of me

And how much he really cares

Is it wrong to feel this lonely

Or to want to have someone close

When all I need is comfort

To make this bud bloom back to a rose

Why do I have to feel

So much pain

These thoughts cross my mind

Again and again

I keep thinking

The words are untrue

I keep disbelieving

The words, I love you

I am beginning to believe

He has someone else in mind

Or maybe he's unhappy

And it's someone else to find

I keep believing

He is going to cheat

When I start to think that

My heart slowly beats

Why do I have to

Feel this way

All I long for

Are happier days

I wish there was something

To fix this strain

To stop my heart

From feeling such pain


I get the feeling

He wants someone else

That I am undesirable

Just when I started believing in myself


Why do I put myself

Through so much pain

I think of suicide

Again and again


I don't deserve this

Nothing at all

Sometimes I wish

Night would fall

And I would never

Wake at all

I am so confused

I don't know what to do


I can't believe him

When he says, I love you

Maybe it's an act

Maybe it's true


But, my dear

I still love you

Another night passes

Yet time stands still

I haven't been the same

Since you left that night

I want to call you everyday

And tell you how I feel

How much I love you

And hug you so tight

I hope you are happy

And free from the pain

I lie awake at night

Thinking of you

Missing you

Wishing you were here


Time stands still

Though life is moving on

There's so much to say

Wishing you were near


I haven't been the same

Since you left all too soon

All the missed experiences

Just brings me to tears


I love you so much, Mom

And will till the end of time

Knowing your spirit will be with me

I never have to fear

There is a hole in my chest and a strain on my heart

I haven't been the same

Since we've been apart

I think of you every night and day

As I sit here

I think of you

Wondering what

You want me to do

I don't understand

What went wrong

It's got me so confused

This has been going on for far too long

There are times when I am with you

I feel so secure

But then there have been times

I am very unsure

I don't know if I'm your girlfriend

Or just a casual fling

I feel like I'm such a fool

For continuing

I know I'm not perfect

And neither are you

I just hate all this frustration

Tell me what you want me to do

I believe I was put here

To bring smiles to people's faces

But never a smile to my own

I guess that explains

The unselfishness and insecurity

And why I am so alone

I've never thought of myself

Without thinking of others first

And when I actually do

It ends up being the worst

I only want to help people

And show that they are loved

With thoughtfulness and caring

Or even a simple hug

When I give myself to someone

I never expect anything in return

For if I do expect the slightest bit

I only end up being hurt

I've always been afraid of falling in love

Since I don't know what to expect

Unfortunately I have let myself

And have become a wreck

I ended up being lied to

And made a fool

But since there was no commitment

There simply were no rules

Feeling betrayed and like a used plaything

From who I thought was my best friend

I have no choice but to think of this

As a "relationship" gone to an end

I've lost that certain part of me

That kept my heart beating so strong

That certain part of me

Which is now a dying song

Why do I feel

He wants someone else

That I am undesirable

Just when I started believing in myself

Why do I put myself

Through so much pain

I think of suicide

Again and again

I don't deserve this

Nothing at all

Sometimes I wish

Night would fall

And never

Wake at all

I am so confused

I don't know what to do

I can't believe

The words I LOVE YOU

Not long ago you held my hand so tight

We would dance in the dark

And kiss by candlelight

But after a short time

We are so far apart

It seems we are so distant

It is tearing up my heart

I lay awake at night

And cry myself to sleep

I wake up in the morning

Only to be disheveled and weak

I keep it all inside

My chest is tight with pain

It hurts me so bad

Because I want it like it used to be

Again

His words burn in my head

As if branded on the brain

How can I resist it

How can I refrain


Why else not

Would the words be true

When so many times

I ended up being the fool


I am at rope's end

Without any slack

To give me the help I need

I should have recovered from awhile back


Images of darkness

Anger and fear

When I look inside

When only a child appears

The lack of love received

And only pain and tears

I am surprised I have lasted so long

After so many agonizing years


I don't believe in love

At least no one loves me

I don't believe there are true feelings

Feeling more worthless than a pea


I think of what is inevitable

What I think could bring me peace

To remove myself from this wretched life

There all pain would cease


I overreact

And create stories in my head

Nothing but negativity

And wishing I were dead

It is not until later

That I realize I was wrong

But then it is too late

Because I am already so far gone


I hate that I feel this way

That my only alternative is death

When really I just wanted peace and happiness

Why does it seem so far-fetched


When I think of negativity

It only seems to justify everything else

I lose all self-confidence

And any caring for myself


It scares me to feel this way

I wish these thoughts would end

Before it gets the worst of me

And I can never come back again

I don't want to die

Or do anything bad

I just hate feeling so lonely

So unloved and sad

Amber liquid flowing through the ice

Trickling down has never been so nice

Oceans of blue seen through the mist

Never realized how much it was sorely missed

More amber flows down feeling warm yet cool

A pretty piece of steel known more than a tool

So shiny and silver reflecting the light

A hint of crimson barely seen

Then flows out so naturally like a gallant stream

What fascinating colors stream down the skin

Never realizing how tender, so delicate and thin

All the pretty colors mesmerize my eyes

As all the colors blur and tantalize

It's too late now; I can't look back

All the pretty colors have faded to black

If I were to describe

What I'm feeling inside

It would be easy to say

I have nothing to hide

But that wouldn't be true

I have to admit

Things are so complicated

It's hard to explain it

I value your kindness

And our conversations on the phone

It's helped me get through times

When I feel so alone

The problem I'm having

Is I am very confused

I've put myself under pressure

And forcing myself to choose

I know it shouldn't be hard

Or seem so demanding

At this moment what I need

Is some care and understanding

As I am driving down this beaten path
I see cars pass by me
I wish I had

There are stops and turns
And flashing red lights
The traffic is stressful
Making my chest feel tight

Up ahead
I see something clear blue
Different streets connecting
And leading to something new

Many exits I pass
Not knowing which one to take
Passing them by may be my biggest mistake

I need to find the map
Which leads the way
To that clear ocean of opportunity
And much happier days

# HOPE and INSPIRATION

When I am in darkness

And despair

Feeling my life

Is going nowhere

When I feel like giving up

Or lost the will to fight

When I'm at my lowest

You are my light

Without even knowing

The troubles I'm going through

They all disappear

Just to talk to you

Your genuine heart

And generous soul

Gives me an instant smile

And makes me feel whole

I thank the universe

And the stars above

For the happiness you give me

And your unconditional love

If I had one wish

I would find a way

To take away

Your pain

I would hold you close

So warm and dear

And wash away

All of your fear

You are always in

My thoughts and prayers

Filled with

Love and care

If there's anything you need

Anything I could do

Just say the word

I'll be there for you

I don't care about
Fame

I don't care about
Followers

I don't care about
Gossip

I don't care about
Narcissism

I don't care about
Superficial

I don't care about
Social media or Tinder

I don't care about
Fairy tales

I care about
Connection

I care about

Animals, environment

I don't care about

Crap food

I don't care about

Religion or race

I care about

Fitness in mind and body

I care about

Wine and laughter

I care about

Spirituality and self-love

I care about

Truth, honesty

I care about

Compassion, empathy

I care about
Family and friendship

I care about
Happiness
.

I care about
Passion

I care about
Second chances

I care about
Dreams

I care about
Connection

I care about
Sex and love

I care about
Making a difference

Time is short

And so am I

So I put on my heels

And enjoy life!

The kindness of strangers

Never ceases to amaze me

The simple smile

Or sweet hello

Fills my insides with an inner glow

Genuine friends

Whether new or old

How they show up unexpectedly

At a crucial time most needed

Realizing you're cared for

To my very best friend

Constant and true

I don't know where I'd be

If I didn't have you

Thank you for being there

Through the laughter and tears

I look forward

To more adventures

In the next 50 years!

I take every day as it goes
And keep fighting for you
Changes happen day by day
This is the best thing to do

I try to understand you
You don't know how hard that can be
To read your mind, what's going on inside
And to know how you feel about me

Your life has complications
As if you're about to go insane
One thing piled over another
But know, you are not to blame

I feel so helpless
I don't know what to do
I want to help you someway, somehow
And stand by you

I'll do anything I can
To help you through these times
I madly truly love you
I'll always be by your side

This last poem has a very special place in my heart, as all of mine do, but this one is extra special. When I was a teenager I learned about this particular musician. The first time I ever saw PURPLE RAIN I was sold, done, absolutely in awe. PRINCE became an enormous part of my life. I was such an obsessive fan I would write lyrics of his songs on my book covers in high school, and for friends as well. Turns out I had a reputation, when someone would ask, "Do you know Kim Farris?" "Oh the girl who likes Prince?"

Yeah, that was me. All throughout high school, college, and beyond, Prince was there for me. His music helped me through my depression and my happiness. I could listen to him for hours and watch his music videos for days.

Years ago, I think in the year 2000, I had an amazing experience. I had the opportunity to go backstage to Prince's show in Irvine! It was a connection I had with an employer at that time. (Darrel Hays, I will never be able to thank you enough for that opportunity). Long story, as short as I can make it, Prince was inaccessible. He had private security; no one can visit whatsoever. Looking at the silver lining, I felt, hey I made it this far. Pretty darn impressive. But then it happened. As I was talking with a gentleman I happened to turn my head. And there he was, walking toward my direction. "Oh, sh** , there he is!" I thought to myself. My heart started pounding, my hands started shaking. "Be cool, be cool. Just acknowledge me, just acknowledge me," I told myself.

And then THIS happened. Prince was walking toward my direction and stopped. RIGHT IN FRONT OF ME. He looked me in the eyes and said, "Hi". I gulped, "Hi". He smirked and made that laugh sound which was always so adorable. I was in shock. Completely star struck, and I don't get star struck. But this wasn't just anybody. This was PRINCE. The man who changed my life.

April 21, 2016 Prince passed.  It was very, very hard to accept, and at times still is.  I am forever grateful for his music and inspiration, entertainment, and just making me smile no matter what mood I was in.

This poem was what I wrote for him after that life-altering event in Irvine.  Unfortunately, I was too scared to send it to him.

U passed by me
My heart skipped a beat
I was in shock; I was speechless
Hoping at least our eyes would meet
And when they did
Oh, what a rush
I felt my whole body
Quiver and blush

U passed by me
The girl with flowers in her hand
Someone U don't even know
But hoped you'd understand
You've inspired my life
At a time gave me reason 2 live
U made me smile
When I felt I had nothing left 2 give

U passed by me
It is only the start
All of what I say
Comes straight from the heart
Your music touches me
Invigoration and happiness U send
I hope that someday
I will be your friend

U passed right by me
We were face 2 face
And said hello
A memory that will never erase

My final words are this:  DO IT

If it makes you happy
It makes you feel good
Don't care what ANYONE thinks
Do what you love
Don't not do something you want to do because of someone
else
Smile more
Love more
Dance
Put yourself first always
Do not allow or react to negative words, attitude or energy-
brush it off immediately
Avoid jealousy
Don't kiss anyone's ass or look for approval
You look amazing
You have a good heart
Caring
Beautiful inside and out
Trust your heart
No matter how you are treated remind yourself you are loved
and should always be happy
Don't strive for perfection, but strive for as perfect as you can
be
Jealousy and inferiority, overthinking, creating stories in your
head are demons-do not let them in
Be yourself, love yourself
The universe is on your side
It can be a pretty cool place if you let it.


                    All my love,
                    *Kim Marie Farris*

# ABOUT THE AUTHOR

My name is Kim Marie Farris. I was born and raised in San Jose, California. I currently live in Los Angeles with my two retired rescued race dog greyhounds, Daisy and Smokey. I thoroughly enjoyed writing as a kid in grammar school, and I remember many times writing "to be continued in my next book" at the end of my short stories! I started writing poetry in high school and have continued ever since. In 2004 I was (and still am) a big fan of Harry Potter and was fortunate to be a contributing writer for the website DanRadcliffe.com. During that time I began to write for the sister site acedmagazine.com. My work consisted of music reviews, interviews with musicians , writers, and celebrities such as Danny Elfman, Tim Burton and Edward Burns. My work also consisted of short stories, poetry, special events and segments on health issues such as eating disorders. I met some incredible people along the way and I am still friends with many of them to this day.

Writing has always been an outlet for me. The poetry I have written spans over 30 years of love, heartaches, depression, and self-reflection. I am a middle child of three and a Pisces. I can identify with the "middle child syndrome" growing up, but thanks to my Piscean imagination and escapism, writing was something I always know where to turn. My goal is not about self-gratification. I am hoping my words touch the reader is some way that resonates, they can relate to and perhaps inspire and uplift them.

My Mother was my biggest fan of my writing. For years she would ask me when I was going to publish my work. I would have one excuse after another. I finally got the courage and confidence to follow through. I promised her I would finish this book and share it with the world. She was so proud of me. My mother passed away January 13, 2017 due to carcinosarcoma. I love you, Mom and miss you terribly. Thank you for believing in me.

54621704R10049

Made in the USA
San Bernardino,
CA